Celebrations

Let's Get Ready for Christmas

By Joanne Winne

Children's Press
A Division of Scholastic Inc.
New York / Toronto / London / Auckland / Sydney
Mexico City / New Delhi / Hong Kong
Danbury, Connecticut

Photo Credits: Cover and all photos by Maura Boruchow
Contributing Editor: Jennifer Silate
Book Design: Victoria Johnson

Visit Children's Press on the Internet at:
http://publishing.grolier.com

Library of Congress Cataloging-in-Publication Data

Winne, Joanne.
  Let's celebrate Christmas/ by Joanne Winne.
    p. cm. -- (Celebrations)
  Includes bibliographical references and index.
  ISBN 0-516-23171-5 (lib. bdg.) -- ISBN 0-516-29567-5 (pbk.)
  1. Christmas--Juvenile literature. [1. Christmas. 2. Holidays.] I. Title.
  II. Celebrations (Children's Press)

  GT4985.5 .W56 2001
  394.2663--dc21

                                                2001017452

Contents

We are getting ready for **Christmas**.

We have a Christmas tree.

Everyone helps to **decorate** the tree.

7

When we finish decorating, we turn on the lights.

The tree is very pretty.

9

We bake cookies
for Christmas.

I help decorate the cookies.

Today is December 25.

It is Christmas day!

15

We **celebrate** the birth of Jesus Christ on Christmas.

17

We give each other **gifts** on Christmas.

This gift is for me!

I give a gift to my mom.

Merry Christmas!

New Words

celebrate (**sehl**-uh-brayt) to have a party
or other activity on a special day
Christmas (**krihs**-muhs) December 25, a holiday
celebrating the birth of Jesus Christ
decorate (**dehk**-uh-rayt) to make
something beautiful
gifts (**gihfts**) something that you give to
someone else

To Find Out More

Books
Christmas Around the World
by Mary D. Lankford
William Morrow & Co.

The Christmas Alphabet
by Robert Sabuda
Orchard Books

Web Site
Merry Christmas.com
http://www.merry-christmas.com/kids_zone.htm
On this site you can play games, make gift tags, and learn how to do Christmas crafts.

Index

About the Author
Joanne Winne taught fourth grade for nine years. She currently writes and edits books for children. She lives in Hoboken, New Jersey.

Reading Consultants
Kris Flynn, Coordinator, Small School District Literacy, The San Diego County Office of Education

Shelly Forys, Certified Reading Recovery Specialist, W.J. Zahnow Elementary School, Waterloo, IL

Sue McAdams, Certified Reading Recovery Specialist and Literary Consultant, Dallas, TX